the Rules of Creation

by Lynda Allen illustrations Tarver Harris

The Rules of Creation
By Lynda Allen

Order books from: www.therulesofcreation.com

Copyright © 2014 Lynda Allen
All rights reserved. No part of this book may be reproduced or transmitted in any form or by any means, electronic or mechanical, including photocopying, recording, or by any information storage and retrieval system, without written permission from the author, except for the mandalas at the end of each chapter and brief quotations for purposes of a book review.

Printed in the United States.

Cover design and book layout by Tarver Harris,
www.tarverharrisdesigns.com

Allen, Lynda.
The Rules of Creation/by Lynda Allen.
ISBN-10: 0692255613

ISBN-13: 9780692255612

Table of Contents

Rule Number 1
You are a creator   12

Rule Number 2
You are Love   20

Rule Number 3
Spirit is you and you are Spirit   28

Rule Number 4
Now is the beginning   38

Rule Number 5
The goal is Joy   46

Rule Number 6
Your heart is your compass, your mind is your tool   54

Rule Number 7
Trust the unseen force that guides the compass   62

Rule Number 8
Imagination is the fuel of creation   72

Introduction

The purpose of this book is divine. It is meant to help each heart it touches to begin each day with a smile and with joy, knowing that you are creating each moment from the Divine within yourself. Each day begun that way in one heart, touches another heart and another until all hearts are living their Divinity, and so we are all living heaven on earth. (I say all this knowing that Spirit may yet have another more grand and glorious purpose for this book in addition to this that I have not yet even begun to imagine!)

The name of the Divine is something I'd like to take a moment to address. There are many words used to attempt to name the unnamable. My personal preference is Spirit. You may prefer Great Spirit, Allah, God, Vishnu, or any number of other titles for the Divine. They are all expressions of that Source whom, by whatever name you choose, is a guide to us on our human journey. From my perspective they are all One, as we are all One. That may not be your belief. Whatever your personal belief about it is, my only request is that since something led you to find this book, if you choose to continue reading it, you do so with an open heart knowing that the words flowed from the perspective that all are a manifestation of the One.

There is one more thing about word choice that I wanted to address. It's a question that was presented to me by a friend who knows me well enough to know that I don't generally like to follow rules! Why then The Rules of Creation? The simplest answer is, that is the title they came with and so I never thought twice about it because I have learned to trust the words that move through me. Beyond that, they never felt constraining to me. They always felt like a guide, a demonstration of a path to creation that I could choose to follow or choose not to follow. However, another, very interesting perspective on the word rule was presented to me after a talk I did about the book. The messages from Spirit can come from unlooked for places! A gentleman spoke to me about movement perception and the idea that we need a rule, meaning a line, in order to be able to detect motion. My heart leapt when this was shared with me because I know the forward motion that was created in my life as I worked with these rules. Suddenly, I could see them not only as a guide for growth, but also as a way to gauge that growth or forward movement. As you work with the rules over time you will be able to reflect back on them and gauge how you have progressed from learning them, to practicing and living them. Ultimately, they become simply a way of being.

In working with The Rules of Creation it also might help to know a little bit about how they came into being through me and how I gradually came to practice living them without even realizing it.

I began writing in earnest in March 2003, a year and a half after the events that took place in the United States on September 11, 2001. Until that time I had carried around with me what I can only call a collective sorrow. I had lost no one I knew on that date in 2001, but I could feel the overwhelming sorrow that hung in the air like a mist. Because I was not quite what I would call fully awake at the time (I'm still working on that today) it took me a year and a half before I was willing to really look at the feeling within myself that something was not right. I had no idea what it was though. So I looked around for a way to understand where I was and what I was feeling. That search led me to a process called Spiritual Discernment. It was a wonderfully simple yet profound process of being guided through a series of twelve steps, all of which prompt you to look within. Part of the process is coming up with a question to ask yourself. As I sat with it, the question I heard the most clearly was, what is mine to do to be happy? Little did I know that I wasn't happy at the time, let alone what I wasn't happy about. Even more surprising was the answer I received.

As part of the discernment process you sit in meditation with your question to go into the stillness for an answer. The answer I received was loud and clear and short. It was simply one word; write. I had done some writing to that point, however, I didn't consider myself a writer by any means and I had never in my life written any poetry. (Yet now I have two collections of poetry published.) Despite all that, I sat with the word write and simply did the only thing I could think to do, I said yes. I had no idea how writing had anything to do with me being happy, but I was willing to be willing. That apparently is all it took (Rule 4).

The next day I began to write. The first thing I wrote that morning was called "The Dam that Sorrow Built." It was my first clue that much of what I had been feeling was related to September 11th. The words very much reflected my emotions as both came pouring out onto the page. It wasn't brilliant but it was a beginning. As it turned out it was the beginning of a process that has brought me much joy, peace and insight.

Right from the start, my writing process was about being willing to open up. After nine years I have found that the best description of the process is that I am a chalice that Spirit fills with words. In being open to the process I allow them to overflow and spill out onto the page. I live in gratitude for the process and for my willingness to listen, as it led to the discovery that writing is one of my soul's great joys (Rule 5). My greatest challenge in the process is for my fingers to keep up with the flow of the words.

For me writing comes down to being a good listener. One day in April 2005 I was being a good listener. Up until that point I had spent a lot of time practicing writing by listening. I had gotten good at knowing when my mind was interfering with the flow of the words and trying to shape them. I could recognize it, take a breath and step back to allow the flow to continue (Rule 6). I had written many things that I didn't understand and didn't have a category for. Were they stories? Poetry? Myths? Some of the stories felt autobiographical and yet I know I didn't live them in this life. I wasn't sure, but I just kept writing them anyway and began to learn to share them. Most importantly I had discovered the joy in the process and my heart would rejoice at any opportunity to sit and be open and let the words move through me. Then one day that April I sat down and watched in wonder as the Rules of Creation flowed through me. They were eight simple steps that fit on one page. I could feel instantly the power and truth of the Rules. There was no need to edit them or expand them, they just were.

There is another important thing about my writing process. When I write something that is meant to be shared I have to learn to live it myself first. I think that's why it took eight years before I began to have an inkling that the Rules were now ready to be expanded. It took me one year for each Rule, though I wasn't conscious of that until now. They needed to be deeply rooted within me before I could hear the fullness of them and even today I am still working on living them completely.

The words that came to support each Rule deepened my knowing of them and showed me more practically how to apply them in my life. I offer them here in hopes that they will bring you the same joy and sense of freedom they brought me in truly knowing that I create my life with Spirit.

My dear friend, Christine, used to smile at me any time anyone used the term co-create, because she knew that I never liked that term. It always felt a little bit off to me and left me feeling like I was supposed to be creating with something outside of myself when, in truth, it felt like Spirit was within me (Rule 3). The Rules of Creation challenged me to truly realize that Spirit is within me and when I am creating from love, it is as one with Spirit (Rule 2).

It was from that joy of creation that this book flowed. When I began I didn't know the form it would take (Rule 7). I only knew that the Rules were ready to expand, and expand they did in ways that left me filled with wonder. With a gentle nudge from love, I discovered that the Rules were accompanied by exercises and/or meditations to help anchor them in. And much to my delight I also found there was a mandala for each Rule as well. Much of my journey has been prompted through images which have guided me and brought me to new levels of understanding. So it was quite joyful for me to be able to also open to images that related to the Rules in addition to words.

As my life shifted in the writing and practice of The Rules of Creation, yours will as well. So here is the only disclaimer I will make with this book. Working with these Rules may create shifts in your life. The shifting may feel uncomfortable or even bring up challenging issues. Therefore, I encourage you to do two things as you move through these shifts. First, make it a regular practice to set aside time to be in the stillness with Spirit. Second, have someone to talk to as you move through these shifts, whether that be a trusted friend, a partner, a family member, a spiritual leader or a counselor. It is invaluable to have someone to share and process your journey with as you move forward.

And the invitation is definitely to move forward, yet to move slowly and gently through this book, sitting with the exercises and meditations at the end of each chapter and working with the mandalas over time. Simply trust your heart's pace as you read. The mandalas are not in the intricate, Buddhist tradition. They are meant to be a simple visual representation of each rule that you can draw within, color, paint or whatever you feel called to do to deepen your understanding of the Rules. I encourage you to make copies of the mandalas or to download the pdfs of them from the website (www.therulesofcreation.com), so that you can start fresh with them if you feel called to. There is also space at the end of each chapter for notes so you can capture your thoughts as you experience them and then add to those thoughts as your knowing of the Rules expands. We are all connected to the same source of wisdom (Rule 1) and yet all see it and experience it from a different perspective, so you may have insights that wouldn't occur to me or to another. Trust what you see and hear as you move through this book and share it with others.

May The Rules of Creation be a helpful partner to you, as you create your life from the pure essence of Spirit that you are. I invite you to release with gratitude whatever vision of your life you had before this moment and imagine your life anew through the heart of Spirit (Rule 8).

Acknowledgements

There are many who have helped make this journey possible.

First and foremost, I will joyfully thank Tarver Harris. This book would not have happened so beautifully without her love, insights and many gifts. The images that grace the cover and that accompany each Rule were created by Tarver, who has such a stunning way of saying yes and allowing Spirit to move through her in images. They are perfect partners to the Rules. She also did the layout for the book. She has many gifts and they all flow from love. I am deeply grateful to her.

My very first opportunity to share one of my poems aloud was a great, terrifying leap for me and a turning point, which set me firmly on the path to these Rules. I'm grateful to Rev. Tricia Hamilton Mack and the people of Unity of Fredericksburg Virginia for that opportunity.

The original one page version of The Rules of Creation might never have seen the light of day without the love and friendship of Christine Agnellini. Her belief in the words that move through me has never wavered. She walked side by side with me every step of living these Rules. I wish each soul such a Heartmate upon their journey.

Bill Brooks was instrumental in the creation of this book. His gentle wisdom and inner knowing are a gift in my life. His certainty of the course for this book was a big part of the energy that brought it into this form so quickly. Living these Rules with him in the joyful creation of our life together is one of the great blessings in my life.

I offer my thanks daily to Spirit for the beautiful dance of this life. Thank you for the gift of these words, the ongoing journey to understand and live them and the joy we express together as the words flow.

Dedication

The Rules of Creation are dedicated
to you and the light of the Divine within your heart,
to Jessica and Lucy
who show me the heart of the Divine every day,
and to Christine Thompson.

Rule Number 1

You are a creator. This is the most important rule; all the others are insignificant if you don't know this rule. You create your life. You create your world. You came here as a creator and you have been creating your life since the day you were born.

Your life is a gift of creation. When you enter this life you enter it with all the power of creation within you. You are born as an acorn, with all that you need to become a beautiful expression of yourself found within. You are born knowing your connection to Spirit, knowing that there is no separation, only oneness. You still know all this, you still have within you all that you need to create the life of your most beautiful and loving expression.

You must first leave behind your ideas of creation. You are breaking no rules, you are not self aggrandizing. On the contrary, you are honoring a simple truth about yourself. You are a creator. Say it, "I am a creator. I create my life."

"I am a creator. I create my life."

You may ask but what about the dire circumstances I find myself in? Did I create that? I would only ask you to look at the lives of others who have been in dire circumstances and who have remembered that truth within themselves. No matter your circumstances you can create anew in any moment.

The key for pure creation is where you create from. A life created from fear and from the mind will look one way. A life created from the heart and the wisdom within it will look another way. You have the power to create either way. Your life is yours to live and to create.

Some as they are remembering that they create their life, feel it as a great responsibility and feel guilt for what they have created so far. But you can see it differently. It is not a responsibility but rather a gift.

There is absolute freedom in the knowing that you are a creator,
that you are connected in each moment with God and unending
love and wisdom.

God and unending love and wisdom.

Sit with that for a moment. You are connected in each moment with
God and unending love and wisdom.

There is nothing you can't know or do or imagine
and so make real. You are a creator and you
can create from unending love and wisdom.
Imagine a world where we all create that way.
How beautiful!

Rule 1 You are a creator.

Introduction to Meditation: Our work with the first Rule begins simply, with only a meditation. Our goal is to relax into these two knowings from Rule 1: you are connected in each moment with God and you are connected in each moment with unending love and wisdom.

MEDITATION: To begin your meditation move to a place you find comfortable for going into the stillness, whether that is indoors or outdoors. Enter into whatever meditation practice you use and settle into the stillness, the deep stillness of the void from which All originates. Take your time getting there; allow your body to be physically comfortable. Acknowledge whatever thoughts arise and allow them to drift away like clouds on a gentle breeze. Breathe deeply until you can feel your whole body is still and at peace.

You are connected in each moment with God. Breathe deeply into your heart and allow it to expand enough to hold that thought. You are connected right now with God. Even as you are reading these words and feeling their meaning, you are experiencing them with the presence of God. God is present with you in this moment. You are breathing in this knowing with God and that presence of God enables you to open your heart wide enough to hold and know that presence within your human expression.

Be still until you feel comfortable with that presence with and within you. This may take time; seconds, minutes, days, years, it doesn't matter how long. You were born knowing the presence of God within you, that knowing still remains, but you must allow time for the reconnection with that knowing. It is important to take this time to anchor in that knowing, that memory of your oneness with God. Once that knowing is anchored in it will serve as a pathway back to that connection in times of forgetting. Enjoy as much time in the stillness as you need in order to be reunited with the presence of God.

You are connected in each moment with unending love and wisdom. Continue to breathe deeply into your heart and still your mind. From within you radiates unending love and wisdom. There is nothing that can stop the flow of that love and wisdom except your own thoughts. Be still and allow any of those limiting thoughts that would contradict this statement to arise. When they do arise, acknowledge them, understand that they no longer hold any power over you, bless them for the lessons they provided and release them with love. Repeat this process for any doubting and limiting thoughts that arise. Remember that you have the inexhaustible love and wisdom to release them and move on without them.

Once your thoughts have become still allow that love to flow forth from you. Smile at the knowing that you are a source of love in the world right now. You are a source of love in the world right now. Let love overflow from your being and move gently out into the world, knowing that as it flows it has the potential to touch each heart on the planet with love. Really imagine that, each heart on the planet being touched by love that flows freely and endlessly from God through you. Sit with that feeling.

Now connect with the deep well of wisdom that lies within you. Let go of any preconceived ideas you have about wisdom. It does not depend only upon the education you have received. True wisdom comes from the heart. This unending wisdom that you are connected to is intertwined with the love now flowing from you. Love knows a deeper wisdom than just what is learned in books.

Imagine a world where you and all others make daily choices from that kind of wisdom, a wisdom based in love. What a glorious world we can create together with the presence of God and limitless love and wisdom.

When you feel your time in the stillness of meditation is complete, return your attention gently to your surroundings.

Rule 1 You are a creator.

MANDALA:

THOUGHTS AND INSPIRATION:

Rule Number 2

You are Love. At the center of your being, of your soul, exists only the energy of Love. There is no fear, no doubt, no hatred, no self-loathing, no separation, no prejudice, and no judgment at the center of your being. Those are all layers that you have created in your lifetime and put on over your soul. When Love is forced to travel through these layers it becomes distorted. Your soul is always striving to throw off those layers and express its true self; Love. Let it.

Yes, it really is as simple as that: Let it. The first step is willingness. Even if you don't feel the willingness in your mind yet, speak the word, yes, anyway. It has amazing power to bring you along with it until you truly are willing. Yes, I am a creator. Yes, I am Love. Yes. Say yes to the truth of who you are and you will be guided to live it.

Yes, I am a creator. Yes, I am Love.

It may feel strange at first to believe that you are love. You have likely spent much of your life not knowing this consciously. You have been taught that love is conditional, that love can be scary or risky, that you should be guarded about loving others. This thinking may take time to overcome. The truth though is that you are indeed love. At the core of who you are is love, for God is love.

Let's clear up another misconception about love. There really isn't something called unconditional love. There is no need to qualify love. All love is unconditional or it is not truly love. There are no terms to love. There is no danger in loving. There is no limit to the amount of love available in the Universe. All are worthy of love. Love flowing freely from the Source is boundless, has no conditions and touches all equally.

A beautiful thing about that love is that it resides within you. It resides within all, not just humans but rocks, stars, trees, animals, sand, air, planets, insects, water, within all. The center of all things is love. If you are still and connected with that love at your core you will feel it in everything around you as well. Everyone has access to that connection, whether they choose to feel it and allow it to guide them or not.

First, connect with the truth and limitlessness of that love within you. Be still and know you are love. Then live from there.

Rule 2 You are Love.

Introduction to Exercise and Meditation: *The goal of both this exercise and meditation is to help with living the last two sentences of Rule 2. The first step is to be still and truly know you are love. The second step is to live from that knowing.*

Sometimes though seeing ourselves as love and worthy of love and truly loving this being that we are, are the most difficult things to do. Therefore, this practice begins and ends with seeing the love you are, with a meditation in the middle to help allow that love to flow.

PART 1 OF EXERCISE: This is a deceptively simple exercise. I know it is because I've done it myself. Put this book down and go sit or stand or lay down in front of a mirror and look at yourself with love. Don't look at the negatives you might normally automatically search for when you look in the mirror; a hair (or many hairs!) out of place, a wrinkle, a crooked smile, freckles, a blemish, a pound or two you'd like to lose. These are the things we have trained ourselves to look for. In this exercise you must look beyond those things. It will take time. Don't berate yourself if you find yourself drifting back to the "flaws," simply refocus. Look at your eyes. Look at yourself like you would someone who is beloved to you. Look until you feel that sense of the beloved for yourself. This is not about narcissism. It is about letting the layers of self-definition we have built up over the years fall away so we can see the truth of who we are. Allow yourself to look with the eyes of love, the way you would look at a beautiful sunset, simply in awe of the beauty and light you find. Once you have reached that place of feeling and seeing love when you look at yourself move on to the meditation.

MEDITATION: Move to a place you find comfortable for meditation, whether that is indoors or outdoors, carrying that sense of love you found in the first part of the exercise with you. Enter into whatever meditation practice you use and settle into the stillness, the deep stillness of the void from which All originates. Take your time getting there; allow your body to be physically comfortable. Acknowledge whatever thoughts arise and allow them to drift away like clouds on a gentle breeze. Breathe deeply until you can feel your whole body is still and at peace.

All you need to focus on in your meditation is the feeling of love you connected with when looking into your own eyes. Feel where the love radiates from within your being. Then simply breathe into and out of that place where love resides. With each breath in, expand the place of love within you and allow love to fill you completely. With each breath out, allow that love to move out from you in every direction, overflowing from the core of love within. Simply continue to breathe, expanding and radiating love for the remainder of your meditation time.

When you feel your time in the stillness of meditation is complete, return your attention gently to your surroundings knowing that with each breath love continues to expand and radiate out from your being.

PART 2 OF EXERCISE: Return to your place in front of the mirror and with the love that you are still radiating from you, look again at yourself. You will be surprised at the difference you see and feel. Now you are seeing with the eyes of Love. What a gift to give to yourself and each person you meet.

This is how we get to the last two sentences in Rule 2: Be still and know you are love. Then live from there. Once you are seeing through the eyes of Love, you live from there; seeing the world and all you interact with differently.

Rule 2 You are Love.

MANDALA:

THOUGHTS AND INSPIRATIONS:

Rule Number 3

Spirit is you and you are Spirit

(or God is you and you are God). Don't scoff, that is simply one of the layers from Rule 2 speaking. Listen to the core of Love, for that is where you and Spirit are One. Spirit resides within you and with you creates your life. Spirit does not judge your creations, you have free will. Spirit simply helps you create what you focus your energy upon. Do not feel guilty or discouraged by what you have created so far. If you do not like the life that you have created then recreate it. If you do like what you have created then share that creation and the process of that creation with others.

The word you use to attempt to name God, Spirit, Allah, is not important, in fact it can be a distraction. There really is no way to utter the true essence of God - how can you speak all that is, in one breath? The answer is simple, you don't speak it, you express it through your being.

Many religions teach that this essence is separate from the human form. While it may be a difficult concept for the human mind to grasp, the truth is that you are God and God is you. At your birth you were a pure expression of the energy of God. Breathe that in, at your birth you were a pure expression of the energy of God.

...a pure expression of the energy of God

Soon after your birth those layers of human thought we talked about in Rule 2 begin to be put on and that pure expression gets filtered through them. Most of the time they are not put on out of malice, but simply because of the beliefs and thought patterns of those around you. Each moment in this journey of your human life is an opportunity to pull off those veils and allow the pure essence of Spirit that you are to flow freely.

The pure essence of the energy of God also expresses as animals and rocks and all expressions of form and matter throughout the Universe. You are not more or less of an expression of God than they are or than any other human being is. You are all expressions of the energy of the One Heart expanding.

What does this mean really? It is actually simpler than it sounds. Everything in the Universe is created from the same source. Period. That source is ever expanding and seeking new forms of expression.

Everything in the Universe is created from the same source.

Because everything is created from that essence of God, everything has within its core all the power and wisdom and knowing of God. Every cell in every expression of matter has all it needs to be exactly, perfectly what it is. Each expression is like the acorn with all it needs to become the oak. Or like the drop of water on Earth with all it needs to become a perfect snowflake and then return again to water. Or like the molecules of carbon in a piece of coal that hold within them the ability to become the diamond. None of these things require a "conscious mind" to live the fullness of the essence of God. Neither do you.

Yet, with that conscious mind you have the opportunity to live in the wonder of creation. You not only have the same ability to create as the acorn, the water droplet or the coal, but you have the added gift of being able to experience wonder in the process of creation.

That act of creation is truly no more than allowing the pure essence of God to flow freely.

You may be wondering, then where does free will come in? You may find the answer to be too simple to believe, though there have been many who have tried to share the knowing. With free will you are given the choice to allow that flow or to filter that flow. Many have used the word surrender to try to describe this process. The problem with that is that people focus on the definition of surrender that means to give up and so see it as a process of giving up part of themselves or something that they love. However, if they focused instead on the definition of surrender that means to give back, they would see the truth of the process more clearly.

...allow that flow or to filter that flow.

For to truly surrender is to give back, in this context it is to give back to the Universe the pure essence of God that you sprung from. By allowing that energy to move freely through you, without those layers and veils, you allow the energy of God to move freely. You allow the natural process of the acorn to occur and so create the oak. The acorn is still part of the process. The creation of the mighty oak still springs from the form of the acorn. You are still part of the creation process of this life you are living, you simply, through free will, get to choose if you will give back to life the pure essence of God or if you will filter it and so stunt its growth and possibly keep it from reaching its full potential beauty.

Unlike the acorn you also have the gift of a conscious mind. Through that gift you can become aware of the veils and see where you may have halted your growth and in each new moment choose differently, choose to allow the pure essence of God that you are to flow. Though some may say that the true gift is with the acorn in that it does not have filters but lives always in the flow. Perhaps if you sit with an acorn you will know the wonder and gifts of the expression of God in each other.

Rule 3 Spirit is you and you are Spirit.

Introduction to Exercise and Meditation: *A good way to move through this exercise is in a tactile way, though that may not be possible in the moment for everyone. As explained in the body of the exercise you can also go through the same process using a visualization. However, my favorite way to do this is with actual pieces or scraps of fabric to represent the veils we are working with releasing. I simply had some fun at the fabric store and bought a yard or two of fabrics that I was drawn to. You can use any type of fabric you like or might already have around your home. You will also need to prepare in advance for the meditation by finding an acorn or any type of seed.*

EXERCISE: We all have those veils whether we are conscious of them or not, whether we put them on ourselves or not. No matter where they originated from, we can absolutely remove them ourselves. Use as many veils/pieces of fabric as you want. I like the gauzy type that you can see through because it reminds me of the layers I see the world through. You don't have to put them over your whole body; it can be enough to put them over one arm and shoulder. The point is to layer the veils on so that you can consciously remove them. You can associate labels with the veils that represent the preconceived ideas you see the world through, like prejudices, religious creed, fear of the other, anger, or labels that have been put on you like parent, son or daughter, teacher, angel, devil, whatever the label, as there are many. If you find the labels distracting feel free to just let the veils be what they are, veils that block you from seeing clearly and block the flow of the energy of Spirit through you. Then breathe deeply and simply remove and let fall each veil one at a time. Take a moment and watch it drop gracefully (or ungracefully) to the floor knowing you are not surrendering a part of yourself but are joyfully opening to allow the essence of Spirit to flow freely from you, freely giving that energy back to the Universe. This is a joyful exercise! Have fun with it!

If the idea of veils doesn't work or you don't have fabric around that you can use, visualization will work as well. Another image you can try working with in place of the veils is the process of a snake shedding its skin. This is a very natural and healthy process for the snake. It enables growth and yet like most things takes a little work. The snake will often have to rub up against something to get all the skin to fall away. Imagine all that serves as a filter over the energy of Spirit that you are, falling away as easily and naturally as the snake's skin.

When you are done with the process, and just before you celebrate your freedom, take a few moments to be still with the feeling of that energy of Spirit flowing freely through you without any obstacles. This is a feeling you want to remember, notice where in your body it seems to move out from. How does it feel? Expansive? Joyous? Breathtaking? Whatever the feeling, take time to be with it and notice everything about it so that it will be easier to return to in moments when you've accidentally picked back up one of those veils. Or like the snake, after you've practiced being in that place of allowing Spirit to express freely through you, you will find that your old skin really wouldn't work for you anymore anyway.

Now celebrate your freedom and the free flowing of the pure essence of God that you sprung from!

MEDITATION: You will need an object for the meditation as well. Find yourself an acorn or any seed. Then move to a place you find comfortable for meditation, whether that is indoors or outdoors. Enter into whatever meditation practice you use and settle into the stillness, the deep stillness of the void from which All originates. Take your time getting there; allow your body to be physically comfortable. Acknowledge whatever thoughts arise and allow them to drift away like clouds on a gentle breeze. Breathe deeply until you can feel your whole body is still and at peace.

Hold the acorn or seed with love and gentleness in the palm of your hand. Feel the power of creation held within that tiny expression of life and feel that same power reflected within yourself. Feel the truth that the acorn has within itself all the wisdom and knowing it needs to become a mighty oak, to be the fullest expression of its being. Feel the same truth within yourself. You have all you need within you to be the fullest expression of your being. Be still and know this simple truth.

When you feel your time in the stillness of meditation with your acorn or seed is complete, return your attention gently to your surroundings.

Rule 3 Spirit is you and you are Spirit.

MANDALA:

THOUGHTS AND INSPIRATIONS:

Rule Number 4

Now is the beginning.

Each moment is a new opportunity for "In the beginning there was…" You create something new each moment. Do not dwell on what you created before or what was created millennia ago. Write your own holy book, your own story. You start with a fresh, blank page each moment. This is the beginning, create.

In one of Earth's holy books, the Old Testament in Hebrew begins with the phrase bereshith, meaning "in beginning." In translation, many add another word to make it "in *the* beginning." The form that can teach us the most though is "in beginning." That is the key, in beginning.

That is the key, in beginning.

In beginning to allow, in beginning to love, in beginning to be, you allow the pure essence of Spirit to express through you. As you choose to allow to give back that pure expression of Spirit through your human form as in Rule 3, you begin to truly create.

To create, from its origins in Latin, means to bring forth. When you are in the moment of now and in the allowing of giving back you are bringing forth the essence of God. Yes, you read that correctly, creation in its purest form is to bring forth the essence of God.

What wonderful things might you create if the energy of God flowed freely through you? Can you feel the joy of that? Many might feel hesitation, fear or even revulsion at the idea of believing they can create with the energy of God.

That is the gift of now. Now is a gift of newness, a gift of birth. In each moment you can choose to allow those layers of fear and old thought patterns that block the flow of creation, to fall away. What if you feel naked and choose to pick up those layers again in a different moment? Even that worry falls away when you remember now. This moment as you are reading these words is the only moment you have. The future is a figment of your imagination and the past is a projection of your memories. Now is all you have. Now is a gift beyond measure. Now is beginning. You can begin this moment, fresh and new and expressing Spirit fully no matter what you believed before now.

Let's be practical for a moment though. How do you begin each moment new? How do you really let those layers fall away? Well, if we carry on with the idea that the phrase is, in beginning rather than in the beginning; then, in the beginning there was the word becomes, in beginning there was the word.

In beginning you have the word and the word is Yes. As we discussed in Rule 2, simply speaking our willingness creates movement. In each moment you can allow the veils to fall and begin creating with Spirit with just the word yes. Yes, I am love, yes I will give back, yes I am a creator, yes, I am God and God is me. With each yes, a veil falls until you are that pure essence of Spirit in expression. In beginning there is the word yes.

> *Simply speaking our willingness creates movement... Yes, I am love, yes I will give back, yes I am a creator, yes, I am God and God is me.*

Your own holy book can be written with only one word. Speak your yes and allow it to guide you as you create now, as you bring forth now in this moment the pure essence of God that you are and create joyfully from there. **This is the beginning, create.**

Rule 4 Now is the beginning.

Introduction to Exercise: *For this exercise you will need to get yourself a journal, or use a notepad like a journal, and get a pen you really like the feel and color of. It will help if the journal or notepad is a size you can carry with you anywhere. This is an ongoing exercise that you can do every day.*

EXERCISE: *This journal is your own personal holy book. Begin each day by writing down the day and date at the top of a blank page. Beneath it write the word Yes. That is all you have to write each day, one word, Yes. You may be tempted to write more, if it distracts you from, or qualifies your Yes then resist the temptation. Carry your holy book with you. If your day does not go smoothly (as they sometimes do) and you find yourself in a place of forgetting and you find yourself saying no, take out your book and write your Yes again.*

Each new day is a blank slate for your Yes. Each new moment is a blank slate for your Yes. Take note of whether your Yes gets easier to write or perhaps gets more difficult to write on certain days. There have been many days when I spoke my Yes through gritted teeth. Don't worry about that, speak it anyway. Remember there will also be days when you sing your Yes joyfully! We are working toward each moment being like that, your Yes is your practice that moves you toward that goal.

Introduction to Meditation: *This meditation is one I did willingly and on blind faith years ago. I'd like to share it with you because it changed my life, but it requires some explanation. It is for you even if you think you already have an open heart, because I thought I did too at the time.*

I was sitting quietly in meditation one day when I heard quite clearly that it was time to take the door of my heart off, hinges and all, and lay it aside. I didn't think about the meaning or ramifications or apparent strangeness. I practiced Rule 4 and simply said yes. I then proceeded to sit with my eyes closed and physically mimed going through the motions of picking up a screwdriver and removing the screws from the hinges on the door of my heart. I removed them slowly and methodically one at a time. I set them on the ground beside me. Then I removed the door with the hinges still attached and also set it aside on the ground. I then sat very still with my wide open heart. It was a strange sensation. **The door is gone to this day and what a joy it is to live with an open heart!**

There were moments that were challenging of course, but I will share with you the guidance I received that made it easier. Not long after doing the meditation I was feeling the discomfort that accompanied this new way of living and I had a frank discussion with God about it. I said, "It feels strange, even risky walking around with my heart wide open. What if it falls out?" The response was simple and profound, "Good. Watch where it falls because Love will grow there." What could I possibly say in response to that other than yes?

MEDITATION: Move to a place you find comfortable for meditation, whether that is indoors or outdoors. Enter into whatever meditation practice you use and settle into the stillness, the deep stillness of the void from which All originates. Take your time getting there; allow your body to be physically comfortable. Acknowledge whatever thoughts arise and allow them to drift away like clouds on a gentle breeze. Breathe deeply until you can feel your whole body is still and at peace.

As you continue in the stillness visualize yourself willingly removing the door of your heart. Picture yourself picking up the screwdriver. Then, one by one gently remove each screw from each hinge that attaches the door to your heart. Imagine yourself placing each screw lovingly on the ground. Then visualize yourself gently and with reverence removing the door that covers your heart, hinges and all, and setting it with gratitude upon the ground. Breathe deeply.

Feel the emotions that may come with the sensation of your wide open heart. Simply acknowledge them whether they are joy, fear, freedom or bliss. Allow whatever emotions arise to simply be there.

Continue to breathe deeply through your open heart with love flowing freely without barriers.

When you reach a comfort level with the feeling of your heart being fully open, return your attention gently to your surroundings. As you move forward from this moment remind yourself that this may be a new sensation and might take some getting used to, but that in the days and years that follow you will sit in wonder at the love that will grow from your wide open heart.

Rule 4 Now is the beginning.

MANDALA:

THOUGHTS AND INSPIRATIONS:

Rule Number 5

The goal is Joy. The goal of life is to live in Joy. Everything you create in each moment should bring you Joy, should lead to Joy, should share Joy with others. You are here to create Joy. Your heart calls out to you each day to live in Joy. Are you listening? Pay attention. Your heart knows the way to Joy. Follow it. Your soul's purpose on this Earth is to create and live in Joy. You each have different gifts for achieving this goal but the goal is the same for each soul; Joy.

What are the unique gifts that God expresses through you? How would it feel to live those gifts fully? If you are a musician, write your symphony with God's notes. If you are a painter, paint your masterpiece with God's vast array of colors. If you are a teacher, inspire your students with the wisdom and knowing of God. If you are a writer, write the heart of God. If you are a parent, see God in your children. If you are a minister, speak with the breath of God. All you do that is an expression of your soul's joy, you are doing from the essence of Spirit.

Have you heard the saying, follow your bliss? This is sometimes written off as some silly New Age thought and yet is an essential truth. Bliss or joy is the vibration of God in expression. It is the name for the human feeling that accompanies the pure expression of Spirit. In very human terms it is the alarm that goes off on the metal detector when treasure is found. Your joy, your bliss is the signal that goes off within your heart when God is flowing freely through you. It is a sure and true guide.

...joy is the vibration of God in expression

This is not the fluttering, ungrounded joy that you can feel outside of yourself. This is the deep and abiding joy that is grounded in the peace of knowing. It is a joy that sustains because of that grounding, unlike the scattered joy that quickly dissipates. You will come to recognize the difference the more you practice feeling and following your joy.

Once you feel that signal within yourself, let it be your guide in relationships, in work, in play, in every aspect of your life. At first you can take one step at a time very slowly, first facing one direction and then another until you feel which one resonates with that joy. Then step with certainty and well yes, joy, in that direction. Before long you will find that your steps won't be as hesitant. You will recognize the feeling of bliss and you will indeed be able to follow it with ease. It will lead you to the next step and the next, until you find that you are gliding through life in a graceful dance with Spirit as your partner.

> *You will recognize the feeling of bliss and you will indeed be able to follow it with ease.*

As you give forth the gifts of Spirit through you in your joyful dance, you share that joy with others. For truly our joy is not just our own. Have you ever smiled at the sound of the pure laughter of children, that giggle of sheer joy? Without knowing it, the purity of their expression of joy touched your heart and you recognized that signal of God within yourself. Your joy serves as the same reminder to others. Your giggle may come in the form of that breathtaking painting or sweeping symphony, or kind gesture, whatever its form it is the essence of God in expression and it is felt by all. Each moment of creation from joy, creates joy for all. Together then, we begin to live nirvana, to live heaven on Earth, now through joy.

Rule 5 The goal is Joy.

Introduction to Meditation and Exercise: Sometimes we don't quite know what our joy in expression is like because we haven't connected with it yet or maybe we haven't in a while or we just can't remember what that joy feels like in our body. Therefore, the goal of both the exercise and meditation is to connect with the feeling of joy and with the pure expression of your soul's joy, remembering or perhaps learning what they both feel like within yourself.

I didn't know that writing was an expression of my soul's joy until I was going through a spiritual discernment process and asked myself the question, what is mine to do to be happy? When I meditated upon that question, the answer was a single word: write. I had no idea what that meant because I was not a writer. At that moment all I could do was practice Rule 4 and say Yes. I started writing the very next day. It was a miraculous transformation for me and it came from an open heart and deep listening to my soul and the joy it wanted to freely express. Now I can clearly see that it is a process that is absolutely an expression of my soul's delight!

You will need a pen and paper nearby to use after your meditation.

EXERCISE: The first step then is to connect with joy and what it feels like in the body. This is definitely a doing sort of exercise. What do you do that is joyful for you? Dancing? Singing? Then put on your favorite song, crank it up loud and dance to your heart's delight or sing with all your might! Do you paint? Get out a fresh canvas and explore some new colors. Do you write? Get a blank piece of paper and let the words flow from joy. Do you find joy in physical exercise? Then as you run, walk, swim or ride focus on each movement being an expression of joy. Whatever it is you do that is an expression of joy for you, let that be your exercise today.

The goal is to really connect with that feeling and vibration of joy within yourself. Take note of where it radiates from within your body. Notice how it makes you feel. Let that joy fill your whole being. Observe the feeling of the vibration of pure joy!

MEDITATION: Move to a place you find comfortable for meditation, whether that is indoors or outdoors. Enter into whatever meditation practice you use and settle into the stillness, the deep stillness of the void from which All originates. Take your time getting there; allow your body to be physically comfortable. Acknowledge whatever thoughts arise and allow them to drift away like clouds on a gentle breeze. Breathe deeply until you can feel your whole body is still and at peace.

In the quiet of meditation sit with the question, what is mine to do to express my soul's joy? It may seem a simple query, but it requires a depth of stillness and a willingness to listen deeply to the stirrings of your soul. Ask this question of yourself even if you already connect with an expression of your soul's joy, for this will be an invitation to go deeper or fly higher upon the wings of that joy.

Whatever it is that your soul whispers to you, listen. It may be one word as it was for me, or it may be a symphony! While still in a meditative state, write down the answer you receive whether it makes sense to you or not. Write it down and with that paper in your hands feel that openness of your heart and say Yes. Say Yes, to that expression of your soul's joy through you.

When you feel your time in the stillness of meditation is complete, return your attention gently to your surroundings.

What you then do with the piece of paper is up to you. You can place it on your altar, hang it up somewhere where you will see it every day, or even burn it so the prayer contained within it will be released. Do with it whatever feels joyful to you. Then go forward with willingness and experience with joy what unfolds.

Rule 5 The goal is Joy.

MANDALA:

THOUGHTS AND INSPIRATIONS:

Rule Number 6

Your heart is your compass; your mind is your tool. Your heart knows all these rules. Your head doesn't believe them. Even now your head is questioning what you are reading. You need only remember that your mind is your tool, a gift for you to use, it need not control your actions. The mind is directly linked to the ego, to the personality of this human existence. The heart is directly linked to the soul. That is why intuition comes from the heart and doubt comes from the mind. Let your heart guide you home and you will live in Joy.

The majority of humans have become a thought oriented race; we have learned to evaluate, to think logically about everything we come into contact with. You have been taught to begin with the mind. Logic and thought are not bad of course, but they are not the only, or even the best method, of finding our way through this life. Our minds are a beautiful and miraculous thing. Mine enables me to write these words. However the words do not come from my mind, they come through my mind from my heart.

Not only can the mind work in beautiful harmony with the heart, it is meant to. The heart is meant to be your guide. You have all you need to follow its guidance. You need only focus on that signal you feel there.

Sounds easy right? But if you've been raised to always start from the mind how do you make the shift to the heart? The first step in achieving that shift is to remember that the mind need not control your actions; it is simply an instrument of this human existence. That may be a new way of living for many, but your thoughts can absolutely be guided by the knowing of your heart. And truly it need not be a difficult shift.

Start allowing your mind to be your partner by using it to think of your heart as your compass. The origin of the word compass is found in Latin and the words com, meaning together and passus, meaning a step. How beautiful. Together you make a step. Together with your heart you make steps.

Begin practicing focusing your attention on your heart and the signal there. Do something that you know always enables you to feel that closeness with God. Then pay attention to how that feels in your heart, learn to recognize that feeling of the flow of Spirit through your heart. That is the magnetic pull of the compass. Stay in that feeling as long as you can so that it becomes a conscious memory. It is a pathway that you are creating, a pathway for your mind to follow that leads to the heart. Then when you are going about your daily life you can recall that memory, that feeling of closeness with Spirit and it will return your focus to your heart.

> *It is a pathway that you are creating, a pathway for your mind to follow that leads to the heart.*

In any moment when you need it, that pull of the compass can be felt. Try it in the middle of your day. Simply stop what you are doing and allow your focus to be upon your heart, open and flowing. If you do, you can feel that energy, that vibration, that homing signal emanating from your heart. Soon you will not have to think about focusing on your heart for it will become a natural way of being; the flow of your life will naturally begin with the heart and move out from there. The flow of creation in your life will then move from the heart to its miraculous partner the mind.

Rule 6 Your heart is your compass; your mind is your tool.

Introduction to Meditation: The first step in allowing the heart to be your guide is to focus upon the heart itself, allowing your attention to be completely on the heart. That then is the goal of this meditation; to focus upon the heart. It is a simple idea, but is vitally important, so important that there is no exercise for this Rule.

How often during your day do you normally pause to focus on your heart? Rarely, if ever? Maybe when it is racing due to exercise or fear? This simple practice can help you return your focus to your heart anytime, in any moment.

MEDITATION: Move to a place you find comfortable for meditation, whether that is indoors or outdoors. Enter into whatever meditation practice you use and settle into the stillness, the deep stillness of the void from which All originates. Take your time getting there; allow your body to be physically comfortable. Acknowledge whatever thoughts arise and allow them to drift away like clouds on a gentle breeze. Breathe deeply until you can feel your whole body is still and at peace.

Continue breathing deeply until you become still enough to feel your own heart beating. That's all; simply slow your breath, let your thoughts rest, and focus all your attention upon your human heart until you can feel the expansion and contraction of it within your chest. If you have never tried this before, it may take a little time. If you have trouble with it the first time or two, put a hand over your heart to make it a little easier to feel its beat. With practice that will become unnecessary.

Once you can feel your heart beating continue in the stillness until you can feel the pulse and energy of your heartbeat throughout your body. Feel the energy that radiates from your heart.

If your attention wanders, simply return it to your heart. Your ego-based mind may want the attention to return to it and the thoughts it is churning out, but simply smile and return your attention to your heart.

The smile is important because this process is about the heart and mind becoming friends and willing partners, the smile is a reminder to the mind about the joy that will be found in working in harmony with the heart. It will help create an essential pathway for your mind to follow that returns it to the heart.

The smile is also a release mechanism for love and joy from the heart. Try it. Notice in the stillness what radiates from your heart when you smile.

This pattern of connecting the heart and mind with love and joy is vital to them working in harmony. Continue to focus upon the beat of your heart with a smile upon your face. When you feel your time in the stillness of meditation is complete, return your attention gently to your surroundings.

Rule 6 Your heart is your compass; your mind is your tool.

MANDALA:

THOUGHTS AND INSPIRATIONS:

Rule Number 7

Trust the unseen force that guides the compass. To be able to follow the guidance of your heart compass you must trust. You must trust the force that guides the compass' point. You do not doubt north when your compass shows it to you, do not doubt Truth when your heart shows it to you. The unseen force that guides the Universe and each heart in it is Spirit, God, Great Spirit, Allah, it has many names but is One and it leads only to Truth. Truth can be distorted by human minds and words and wills which is why you were given a compass to guide you. You need only trust it and the force that guides it. To truly create Joy you must be able to trust the guidance you are given each moment.

Trusting in something you cannot see, some would call that faith, some would call that foolish. Really the only hindrance in trusting in this way takes us back to our partner the mind. In the mind is where the evidence is needed in order to trust, in order to make something real. If we are in our hearts there is no need for proof because from the perspective of the heart there is nothing that is not seen or not known. So in truth there is no need for trust once we have reached a state of living from the heart.

How then do we reach that state and overcome our mind's desire for proof in order to trust? We remember the idea of the compass. If you were in the wilderness and you had nothing to guide you but the compass in your hand, would you trust it when the arrow pointed north? Certainly, because your mind has learned that this is a consistent truth. Why then when you are lost in the wilderness of your life would you look to or trust anything other than your internal compass?

How do we get to trust? How do we truly live the meaning of the compass, to step together? Simple, remember the graceful dance with Spirit that we began when following our joy in Rule 5? To trust we need only look at the steps together as a continuation of that dance with Spirit.

To be good dance partners you must step together in harmony, you must move together as one, you must trust each other. When dance partners trust each other there truly is not one who leads and one who follows, there are just two in the flow the music.

When you falter in your dance is it because you don't trust the notes? Or is it because you don't trust your feet? Your mind questions what your body and heart feel from the music and so your steps falter. When you simply move with the flow of the music the dance finds a natural rhythm and beauty.

It is no different with the compass of your heart. Trust the infinite wisdom of Spirit that guides you as you would trust the music of the waltz or the point of the compass. Then simply step together with Spirit in Divine harmony, in a glorious dance.

"Trust the infinite wisdom of Spirit."

To achieve that state of grace and trust, great dance partners do take time to practice together. This is where the practice of meditation or prayer comes in. Meditation or prayer is a time to practice dancing with your partner. It is a time to be still and feel the flow of the harmony all around you, to sway gently to the music with Spirit. It is a time to become reacquainted with the steps of the dance you came into this world knowing. In the silence you can begin to hear again the music. In the silence you can begin to feel again that connection your heart provides to Spirit. This is your practice time.

As your practice becomes more regular so will your steps become more certain. You will learn to step together in each moment, until your whole life becomes a beautiful expression of the fluid dance of the Divine.

Rule 7 Trust the unseen force that guides the compass.

Introduction to Exercise and Meditation: This exercise is one you might have to do some advance planning for. With the way we often rush through our days it will take a clear intention to live differently for a day. The goal of course, is to live guided by our heart compass every day, but we will begin the practice with just one day, as my friend Janelle did. I'm grateful to her for being part of the inspiration for this exercise. She called it her Universe Day. On a vacation, she set aside one day to listen to and follow the guidance of the Universe in her every choice. She experienced a day filled with joy and wonder.

This exercise is where we get to put many of the earlier practices in this guide to use together. Pick a day during your week that you will set aside to practice letting the unseen force that directs your heart compass guide you, to practice your dance with Spirit. Remember that the word compass from its origins means to step together. So in truth you are setting aside a day to step together with God and to allow God to express freely through you.

If you've never done this before it is best to choose a day when you don't have a lot of what you would call obligations to take care of, but rather a day when you might have a little more freedom to be and go where guided.

Before you rush out into your joyful dance though, it is helpful to begin the day with stillness. That quiet time with Spirit is essential when practicing being guided by your heart compass and stepping together in your dance with Spirit.

In our human expression, learning to trust and follow the guidance of our internal compass and finding your personal indicator of true north are key. Everyone has an arrow within them that will always point them towards truth. Finding your own true north is the goal of this meditation.

The energy of Spirit flows freely through your Divine or unbreakable heart providing the wisdom, love and knowing that direct the arrow. However, where you feel that arrow within your body is unique to you. For myself, I feel the compass needle's point within my heart. Some feel it as a "gut feeling" and so their reference of true north is in the area of the stomach or solar plexus. Still others may feel it in the throat area and so know whether or not they are speaking or feeling truth there. For you to be able to trust your internal compass you must first find your own internal true north.

MEDITATION: Move to a place you find comfortable for meditation, whether that is indoors or outdoors. Enter into whatever meditation practice you use and settle into the stillness, the deep stillness of the void from which All originates. Take your time getting there; allow your body to be physically comfortable. Acknowledge whatever thoughts arise and allow them to drift away like clouds on a gentle breeze. Breathe deeply until you can feel your whole body is still and at peace.

Begin as we did in the meditation for Rule 6 and focus upon your heart until you are still enough to feel its beat within you.

Then, in order to find where true north is within your body, simply think of something you know to be true for yourself. Focus on something you feel as an absolute truth; that can be something as simple as the knowledge that the sun rises in the east and sets in the west or it can be your knowing of your own belief in God. Whatever it is, focus completely on that particular truth. (CONTINUED)

Rule 7 Trust the unseen force that guides the compass. (CONTINUED)

Smile as you allow that truth to radiate from the Divine wisdom of your heart and take note of what direction it flows in your body. That flow is the path of the needle on your compass, it is the direction your arrow points when it finds true north. It is the flow of energy from Spirit which offers guidance to you on this human journey. Continue to focus on that flow of energy along your internal compass needle until you have no doubt where your true north resides within your body.

Allow your mind the time to understand that feeling and remember that path from the core of Spirit to the tip of the compass point. Allow your whole body to become aware of and familiar with that feeling as it is the key to following the guidance of Spirit in each step of the dance.

Feel the truth that to truly trust your compass and so to trust Spirit to guide your steps, is to dance through life with Spirit as your partner.

Then, when you feel your time in the stillness of meditation is complete, return your attention gently to your surroundings. Bring with you the memory of your true north and the knowing that your steps on this day will be guided by the natural flow of the movement of Spirit through you, which creates the beautiful dance that is your life.

EXERCISE: Today is a day for stepping joyfully into the dance, so all you need to bring with you today are your joy and your dancing shoes!

For this one day, do only what feels joyfully guided by Spirit. Allow the vibration of joy that is God in expression to help you follow your compass today. Let it guide you in all your choices from what clothes you put on, to what food you eat, to what activities you do, to whom you spend time with. It can be as simple as walking down the street and pausing to allow joy to guide you as to which street to turn on to, or what store to go into. When making a choice today simply return to the feeling of the needle pointing to true north from your meditation and allow that vibration of Spirit in expression to nudge the needle of your compass to your north. Then follow Spirit's lead in the dance of your day. Listen to and feel the music of the Universe as you dance: with Spirit as the conductor it will guide you gracefully to the treasures the day holds. What you will discover will be beyond anything you could have planned or imagined on your own!

If your mind interferes and guides you in a direction that "makes more sense," let that be ok. Just pause, acknowledge that moment of the mind overruling the heart. This will help you recognize it sooner the next time it happens. Then take a moment to return to your feeling of the compass pointing to true north and simply retrace your steps and go to where your compass wanted to lead you, or ask the question you hesitated to ask, or offer the help you chose not to offer. Whatever it was that your mind led you away from, return to it with your heart wide open.

The goal of this exercise of course, is to help us recognize that feeling of the pure expression of Spirit through us so that we can follow it every day in every circumstance. Imagine that; a whole world full of people living the pure expression of God through them. What could be more joyful?

Rule 7 Trust the unseen force that guides the compass.

MANDALA:

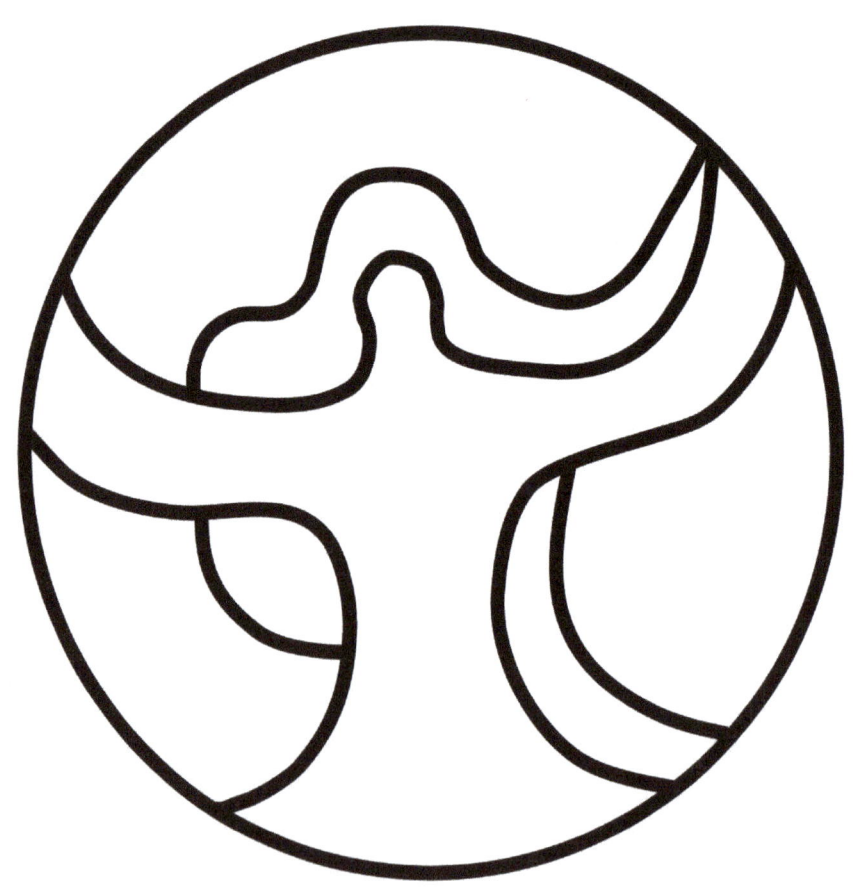

THOUGHTS AND INSPIRATIONS:

Rule Number 8

Imagination is the fuel of creation.
To create a thing or a feeling or a world you must first be able to imagine it. This is where your heart and your mind finally unite and work as one. When they do, true miracles are possible. Imaginings born of the heart and expanded and seen in the mind are the true work of creation. Uniting all the forces of creation through Love and Joy and trust and focusing them with the heart and amplifying them with the mind is your work. Imagine with the Joy of a child all the glorious things the Universe can hold and be. Imagine with all the Love that is at the core of your being. Imagine with all the power of creation behind you and create a world of beauty and Peace and Joy and Freedom.

Once you know the rules of creation the question then becomes, what shall I create in my life and my world? You are limited only by the bounds of your own imagination. You can create anything you can envision. The key is to imagine from that pure essence of God that you are. Imagine from there and you will create the grandest vision of your life. Imagine with the love at the core of your being. Imagine with the gleeful joy of your soul. Imagine from the stillness. Sit at the center of the compass of your heart and allow the vision to come forth from there. Then hold the image of the heart's vision within your miraculous

> *Sit at the center of the compass of your heart and allow the vision to come forth from there.*

mind, see it there in its fullness, in great detail. See it in your mind as Spirit would see it. Then trust the guidance of the compass to lead you in the process of creating in the physical what you imagined with God. Trust the beautiful dance of the Divine and its steps which will lead you to that perfect vision of your life.

Each moment is a new beginning. It is yours to imagine.

Rule 8 Imagination is the fuel of creation

Introduction to Meditation and Exercise: *Set aside a significant block of time for meditation. Take your time and move slowly through the meditation. Have your favorite writing and/or drawing utensil nearby in order to work on the exercise immediately following the meditation.*

MEDITATION: Return then to the stillness, the deep stillness of the void from which All originates. Take your time getting there; allow your body to be physically comfortable. Acknowledge whatever thoughts arise and allow them to drift away like clouds on a gentle breeze. Breathe deeply until you can feel your whole body is still and at peace.

In that haven of stillness, rest. In this moment you are simply resting in the love that is Spirit.

The practices and knowings you have come to are absorbed into your being. They have settled into each cell of your body.

You know that you are the essence of God in expression.
You are ready to live as the creator you are.

This place of stillness and Love is where you live from.
Spirit emanates from this place within you.

From that place of Spirit return to the body of Rule 8 and begin seeing the vision of your life through the eyes of Spirit: Imagine from there and you will create the grandest vision of your life.

Imagine with the love at the core of your being. Imagine with the gleeful joy of your soul. Imagine from the stillness. Sit at the center of the compass of your heart and allow the vision to come forth from there. Then hold the image of the heart's vision within your miraculous mind, see it there in its fullness, in great detail. See it in your mind as Spirit would see it. Then trust the guidance of the compass to lead you in the process of creating in the physical what you imagined with God.

Once the vision is clear in your heart return your focus to the present moment. (Know also that you may gain more clarity or insight on the vision as you continue a regular practice of meditation and allowing Spirit to guide you.)

Exercise: Write down the vision you see on the following pages, or draw it in the blank mandala if it comes in pictures more than words. Then go forth and create it!

Rule 8 Imagination is the fuel of creation.

MANDALA:

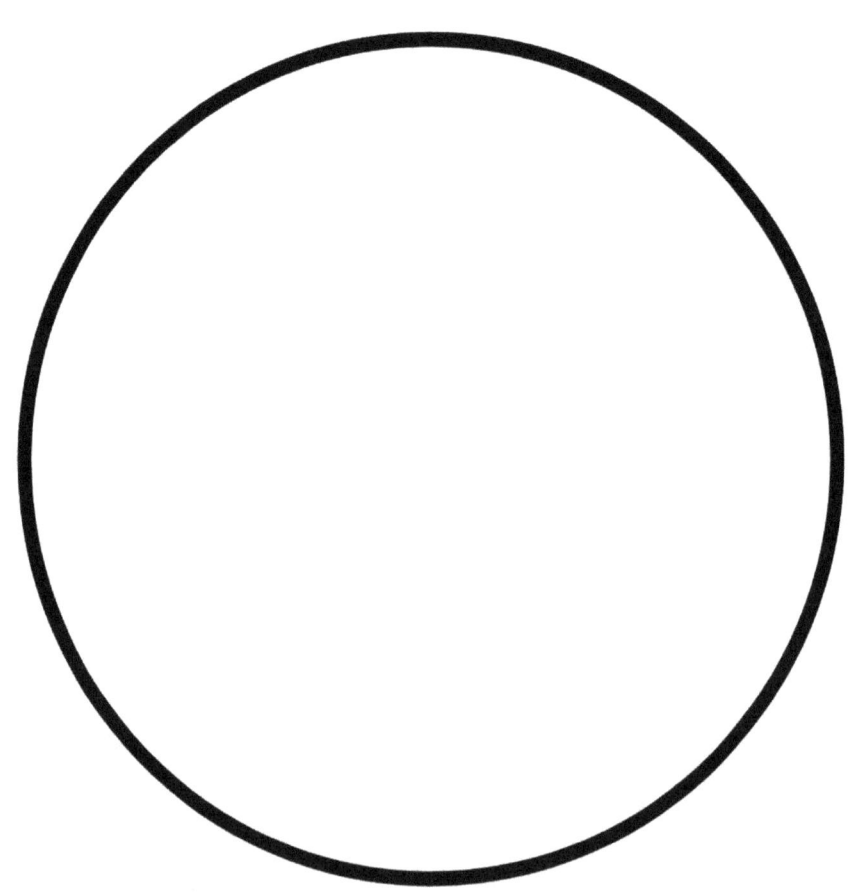

THOUGHTS AND INSPIRATIONS:

Other titles by Lynda Allen

Poetry Collections:

Rest in the Knowing

Illumine

Both available through Peace Evolutions, LLC at www.peace-evolutions.com

Fiction:

Sight to See

Kindle edition available through Amazon.com

www.ingramcontent.com/pod-product-compliance
Lightning Source LLC
Chambersburg PA
CBHW062113290426
44110CB00023B/2800